Observations On The Construction Of Railway Carriages: Together With A Paper On Railways And Their Management

Robert Francis Fairlie

In the interest of creating a more extensive selection of rare historical book reprints, we have chosen to reproduce this title even though it may possibly have occasional imperfections such as missing and blurred pages, missing text, poor pictures, markings, dark backgrounds and other reproduction issues beyond our control. Because this work is culturally important, we have made it available as a part of our commitment to protecting, preserving and promoting the world's literature. Thank you for your understanding.

OBSERVATIONS

ON THE

CONSTRUCTION

OF

RAILWAY CARRIAGES,

TOGETHER WITH A PAPER ON

RAILWAYS AND THEIR MANAGEMENT.

BY

ROBERT F. FAIRLIE, C.E.

LONDON:
PRINTED BY C. WHITING, BEAUFORT HOUSE, STRAND.
1868.

ON THE

CONSTRUCTION OF RAILWAY CARRIAGES.

OBSERVATIONS ON THE DISADVANTAGES OF THE PRESENT SYSTEM OF COUPLING AND BUFFING CARRIAGES AND WAGONS FORMING TRAINS, TOGETHER WITH A DESCRIPTION OF A NEW METHOD OF ACCOMPLISHING THESE OBJECTS.

Passenger Carriages.— Passenger carriages are usually coupled together with screw couplings for the purpose of jamming the buffer-heads together, and thus preventing to a great extent the oscillations that result at high speeds from loose couplings. The close coupling prevents the usual violent pulsations of trains, so disagreeable to passengers when starting or stopping. In many cases, when trains loosely coupled have been started, the passengers have been jerked off their seats.

The carriages in a train, the buffers of which are jammed together in the manner described, run steadier, and are much less affected by the imperfections of the line; and, consequently, so long as the line is straight, the wear and tear of tires and rails is reduced.

On curved lines, however, the disadvantages of tight coupling are found to be very great. The flange friction of a train is greatly increased when passing round curves, because the entire pressure brought on the opposed buffers by means of the screw coupling, which on the straight line is on four buffers, is on a curve removed to the two on the inner side, as shown at A, Fig. 1 ; and the pressure is, moreover, augmented by the opposed ends of the carriages being brought closer together on that side. The whole of this pressure being directly above and in line with the inner rail, its force is directed to press the train outwards against the outer rail—*i. e.*, the train is trying by this amount of pressure to force itself straight, and thus the outside flange friction is very largely increased. Thus we have an artificial force in effect, producing quite as great, if not greater, flange friction than that naturally due to grinding the carriages round the curve, and that due to centrifugal force from velocity. This friction, already much too great, is further augmented by the mode of tying the carriages together by their ends, notwithstanding that many have continuous draw bars attached to them. The ends of the carriages thus tied together extend from 5 to 7 feet beyond the centres of the axles; consequently, on a curve each end must project some distance beyond the centre line of rails to a point between the centre line and the outside rail, as will be seen at B, Fig. 1. The present mode of draught is from the ends of each carriage, the draw hooks being always placed in the centre of the end cross bar of the frames (see B, Fig. 1); the consequence is that the full force of the engine is conveyed through the train in a line of draught outside the centre line between the rails. In other words, each carriage in this manner is pulled against the outside rails, and in turn pulls the next, and so on to the end of the train, thus adding another force to increase flange friction beyond the three just described.

Buffers of the usual form between carriages are often a fruitful source of accident, often resulting in loss of life. It has frequently been remarked after a collision, or other sudden stoppage of a train, that carriages get piled up one on another in a most extraordinary manner, leading almost to the belief that it could only have been done by the use of cranes ; but it is the imperfect contact of the buffers and uneven character of

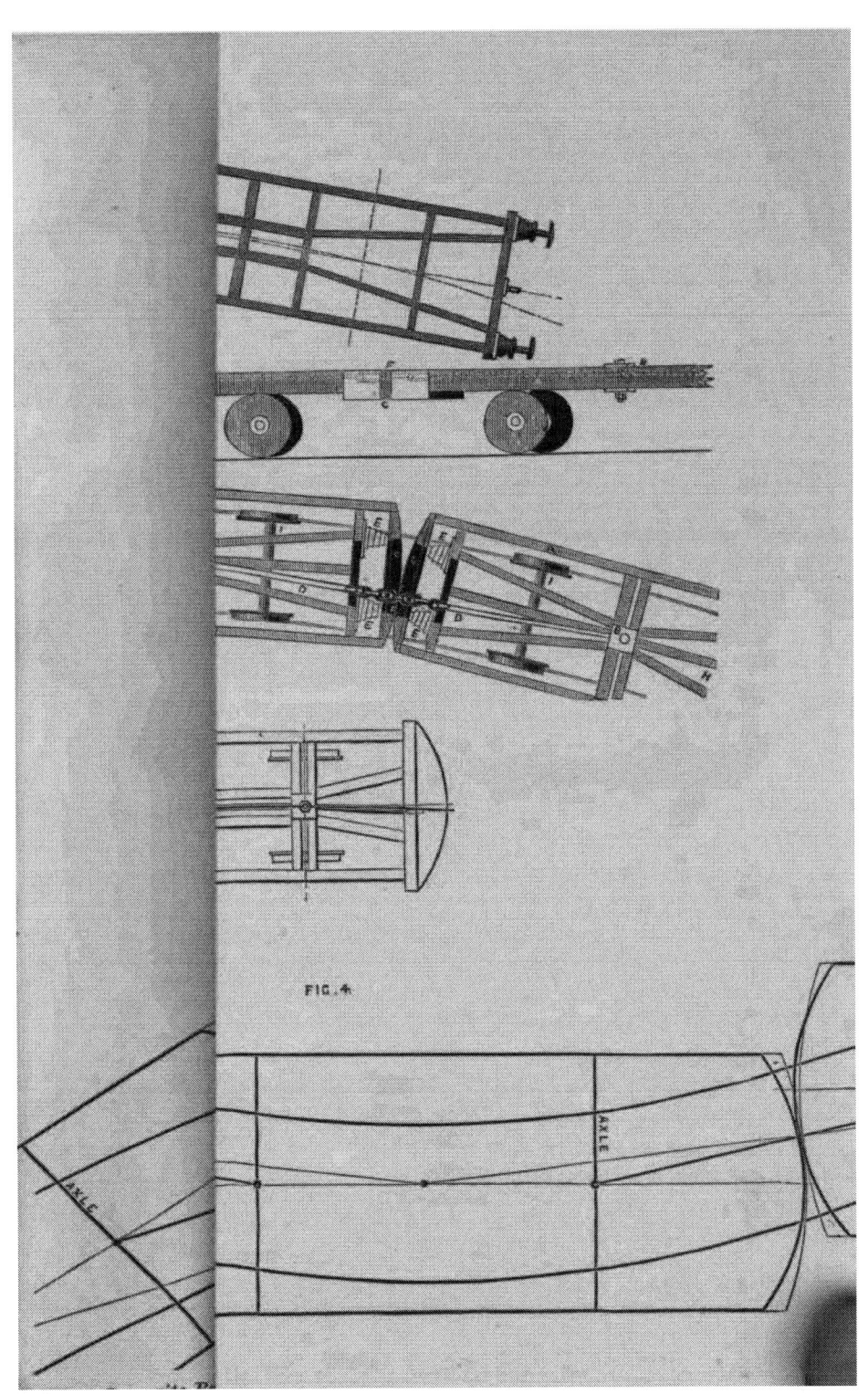
FIG. 4

the buffing springs which cause the buffers to override each other, and consequently mount upwards. Were there no buffers at all, or buffing springs, this would rarely, if ever, happen; because the horizontal force would be resisted by the wagon frames being directly in line, and already rigidly connected with each other. The train would represent one rigid mass longitudinally, each wagon sustaining its proper share of the whole weight, yet with perfectly easy motion to suit curves or reverse curves transversely. Carriages connected together in the present form require to be much stronger, and are consequently much heavier, with the object of resisting the shock and strain thus brought on them. This is especially so on metropolitan lines, where they are compelled to stop and start very quickly, because the stations are so close together.

Wagons.—It is well known to all who have carefully watched merchandise trains, either *en route*, or shunting at stations, or at goods depôts, that an enormous wear and tear must take place by reason of the bumping and checking the wagons receive, this rough usage, in many instances, snapping coupling chains or breaking buffer heads, beside causing a corresponding amount of destruction to the wagon frames, because the force employed to break a coupling or burst a buffer cylinder must first have expended itself on every wagon, the broken coupling or buffer simply showing the weakest point for the time being. Beyond this destruction to stock, there is a corresponding amount of destruction to the contents of the wagons; merchandise gets broken and dislocated; cattle get horribly bumped about and shaken. All who have seen cattle in trucks shunted about stations, must have felt pity for the poor helpless beasts; the bumping and bruising they get is very great, and is, moreover, exceedingly cruel. I have known of beasts being knocked down in the wagons while the others trampled upon them. To make matters worse, cattle are usually placed in the trucks so that they stand transversely to the line of rails, thereby taking away the protection nature has given them by a long base fore and aft to withstand such shocks. This is very important. Owners of cattle must often have noticed a serious depreciation in the value of the animals from this cause. The damage to frail merchandise must also form a very large item in the working expenses, as, no doubt, could be ascertained from the station-masters' accounts; the constantly occurring claims that have to be paid for damaged goods must form a very heavy item in the general charges, which is simply taking money out of the shareholders' pockets. Milk is affected from the same cause, though principally carried by passenger trains. No milkman would send his milk by goods trains, because it would be half churned into butter; therefore this traffic has wholly to be carried in passenger trains, thereby affecting the working expenses. Coal is also very much damaged in transit by reason of loose coupling, so much so that a certain allowance is made by coal owners to the purchasers for lost by breakage, &c., during its railway journey. It frequently happens that large pieces of coal are shaken off the wagon during this process of bumping, and such lumps at times have thrown wagons off the rails. Coupling the wagons together by the present system adds considerably to the length of the train. The buffers extend nearly 2 feet from each wagon, and the space between the buffers is invariably from 6 to 12 inches; thus there is a space of between 4 and 5 feet between each pair of wagons, which is multiplied by the number in the train; this unnecessary length of train adds considerably to its friction on curves, and reduces in proportion the usefulness of the engine. Were we to couple wagons together as we do carriages, engines of the ordinary type could not haul anything like the same number of wagons in each train that they now do, because the flange friction on curves would increase so rapidly that it would soon absorb the whole power of the engine. It is the space between the wagon buffers that is now left which permits trains being worked as at present.

The new mode of coupling, which I shall explain presently, would reduce the flange friction on curves to the minimum, so that the dynamic force required to haul a train round a curve would be very little, if any, more than would be required on a straight line.

The disadvantages attending the present system of coupling carriages and wagons together are enumerated as follows:

1st. Great danger in case of collision.

2nd. Greatly increased flange friction of all trains on curves, and consequent wear and tear.

3rd. Additional strength rendered necessary in the construction of carriage stock, and the proportion of dead to paying load is thus increased.

4th. Heavy items of expenditure caused in the merchandise department through damage to frail goods.

5th. Injury and damage to cattle.

6th. Loss of coal by breakage beyond the expense of screens and re-screening at the end of a journey.

7th. Damage to milk.

8th. Unnecessary length of the trains requiring a corresponding increase of expenditure in siding, station, and goods' shed accommodation.

9th. Great destruction and wear and tear of wagon stock, broken coupling chains, buffers, &c. &c.

On the other hand, the advantages of the new system of coupling, which is illustrated in Figs. 2 and 3, are as follows:

1st. The foregoing disadvantages are entirely avoided, and their consequences saved.

2nd. A great reduction is made in the dead weight of wagons, whilst their strength and usefulness is maintained.

3rd. The life of each wagon is greatly lengthened, and a reduction is made in the cost of repairs by preventing all this bumping and smashing.

4th. A reduction is made in the wear and tear of rails and tires by reducing both vertical and lateral oscillations.

5th. It immensely reduces the flange friction of all trains on curves by fixing the line of traction inside instead of outside the centre line between the rails throughout the entire length of a train, the coupling bars forming the chord of the arc traversed by every two wagons; that is, each wagon being tangential to the curve it is traversing, the coupling bars will form the chord of the curve between the centres of every two wagons. See Figs. 2 and 4.

Where this new system of coupling is adopted the entire power of the engine will be exerted through each wagon in such a manner as to pull the following one away from the outer rail—the exact reverse of the present system; hence the reduction, if not altogether the prevention, of flange friction on curves. Centrifugal force is also partially counteracted in this manner; for instance, a line drawn through the centre of each wagon on a curve from end to end will be tangential to that curve—that is, the centre line so drawn will cross at right angles to a radial line, or line drawn through the centre of a wagon from the centre of the curve, which line represents the direction of centrifugal force, therefore each wagon has through centrifugal force a distinct tendency of its own to fly outwards, the amount of this force being in the known proportion due to the curve and speed. Wagons are much longer than their wheel bases, consequently, when on curves, the centres of the wagons at each end must pass a certain distance in proportion to the curve to the outer side of the centre line between the rails, as shown in Fig. 2; hence the line of traction must be outside the centre line of rails. Now if, instead of coupling wagons at the points just mentioned, we coupled them from centre to centre—*i. e.* at the points where the centre line of each wagon crosses the radial line, a slot being cut in the end pieces to allow the coupling bar to pass to each side of the centre of the wagon frames—it will at once be seen that the coupling bar would form the chord of the circle traversed by every two wagons, and as the tractive force would be through the chord, it follows that its effect would be not only to greatly counteract centrifugal force (and increase to that extent the safety of trains on curves), but the friction due to it would be removed, together with all the other flange frictions which now exist from coupling. The line of traction would be between the centre line of rails and the inner rail, just the reverse of the present system. The wagon frames at each end are curved to a radius drawn from the centre of each wagon; the slotted holes already mentioned are in the curved ends to permit the coupling bar passing to either side of the centre of the end of each wagon. The wagons are all coupled tightly together, so that the movement of the engine alone affects that of the train. Instead of carrying the bars D D to the centre of the framing B B, they may only extend to the centre over each end axle at C C, and the ends be struck from these centres instead of the centres B B. Elasticity may be allowed for in this case the same as in the other. In order to maintain the continuous draw bar throughout the train, a centre bar is placed between the two centres C C, coupling these together, and transmitting the strain throughout the train. (See Fig. 3.)

It is well known that nothing is so beautifully delicate in its movement as an engine passing from rest into motion. Those who may have stood on the foot-plate and started an engine, even without a train, know that it is done in the most easy and graceful manner; therefore by coupling up the train in one solid mass, its movement must be as delicate as that of the engine itself, hence all the damaging effects of the present system are at once removed. At this point the question suggests itself, " Can you get round the curves with a long goods train coupled up tight in this manner?" The answer is " Certainly." Because the ends of each wagon being curved to a radius from the centre, they meet together perfectly in line, whether on a curve or reversed curve, or on the straight—the distance apart from centre to centre remaining always the same. (See Fig. 4.)

Another most essential point is gained by thus keeping the wagons equidistant from each other under all conditions of circumstances, and these are as follows. The necessity for increased adhesion on mountain lines is very great indeed, so much so that all kinds of expedients have been resorted to to overcome the difficulty; but the impossibility of being able to maintain at all times equal the distance between the wheels of the wagons coupled together, has rendered the whole matter so difficult that it has not been accomplished. Patents have been taken out for coupling carriage-wheels together with all sorts of contrivances for allowing the couplings to lengthen or shorten, as curves or the pulsations of trains necessitated; but so far as I know, the matter has never succeeded. Now by my plan the distances apart between the centres of axles of the wagons are always the same, or so nearly always the same, that the difference is inappreciable on curves or reverse curves, and this being so, each axle could be coupled to the next by means of pulleys being fixed on their centres, driven either by plain or ordinary straps or belts, or grooved pulleys may be used with circular ends of any material, or pulleys grooved or plain, reversed or otherwise, for any kind of link—thus at all times, on all conditions of roads, each axle can be made to drive the following one in the way suggested; and in like manner can the retarding movement be effected throughout the entire length of a train from the driver's footplate, as the same element of constant distances at all times between the centres of all the axles in a train is essential for the best application of break power either by Clarke's patent or the ordinary lever and screw break.

RAILWAYS AND THEIR MANAGEMENT.*

THE Society of Arts some years ago took into consideration several popular questions relating to railways, and although, as an engineer, I have other opportunities of drawing the attention of the profession to which I have the honour to belong, to questions of a purely technical character, I desire to bring under discussion at this Society the general subject of railways and their management, in order that something may, if possible, be done towards bringing about a much-desired reformation.

At no period in the history of our railway system could the consideration of the various questions springing out of the subject of this paper have been so appropriately introduced as at the present, when it is remembered that a sum approaching in magnitude to the national debt is involved in their consideration. Probably no less than 20 per cent. of this enormous investment is at this moment wholly unproductive, and surely no question better deserves the most serious consideration of our public men than that of devising some practical remedy for this lamentable condition of railway property, affecting as it does not merely those whose capital is directly invested, but the prosperity of the whole empire, and particularly so in the case of Ireland.

The question of the regeneration of Ireland has for a long period occupied and perplexed the ablest minds in the country. It is neither my desire nor my province to deal with its political condition, but it is impossible to ignore the necessity for dealing with the social and industrial welfare of the people. Everywhere railways have been found among the chief agents of civilisation and the real pacificators of discontent and disaffection. When you make a people wealthy and prosperous,

* Paper read before the Society of Arts, March 18, 1868.

political reforms become of secondary interest, and will find their solution in due time. Ireland is essentially an agricultural country; and however much we may desire to see her advance in commercial and manufacturing progress, neither agricultural prosperity nor commercial success can be expected without an economical and efficient system of railway communication ramifying throughout every district. Much has been said, both in and out of Parliament, respecting the purchase of railways in Ireland. Royal commissions have inquired, select committees have reported, and statesmen of every party have devoted their best attention to this subject; but, after all, we are as far as ever from being agreed as to the policy of that course. I cannot, as a practical man, bring myself to recommend—although much may be said on both sides—an experiment of that speculative character, involving as it does the whole imperial question of Government purchase and management. I hold a decided opinion that it is our duty to assist and hasten the development of Irish resources in every possible manner, and I know of no better plan than that of extending railways throughout every part of the island. This we know cannot be done by private enterprise, because of the unremunerative character of the existing lines, arising mainly from their great cost originally, and from the diversity of control and management. There are extensive districts in Ireland urgently requiring railway communication, which ought to be constructed, alike for the public benefit and the advantage of the existing lines, always providing that the character of the work be good, and the cost moderate, such as to bring them within the scope of remuneration. But whence is to come the means of accomplishing this? I should say, by uniting to urge upon the Government the adoption towards Ireland in this respect of a policy analogous to that which has been so successfully applied to India, where a beneficent system of railway legislation has allayed the spirit of discontent and disloyalty in the growth of material wealth and individual well-being. An imperial guarantee of $3\frac{1}{2}$ per cent.—which would probably not involve the State in a liability of more than 100,000*l.* per annum—would evoke from private sources alone sufficient capital to construct nearly one thousand miles of railway. This would add 50 per cent. of mileage, at a cost (say) of 3000*l.* per mile, which in my judgment is ample, having regard to the circumstances of the country. It is not to be denied that to continue the extravagant system of the past would be no advantage to Ireland.

I will undertake to say that such a guarantee from the Government would only for a comparatively short time remain a burden upon the State finances, provided that the outlay were judicious, and the management adapted to the actual requirements of each particular case.

Railway management in Ireland must surely have reached the height of absurdity, when we find that something under 2000 miles of road are governed by no less than between 30 and 40 different boards of direction. Omitting three or four of the principal lines, the average mileage to each board is not over 25 miles, and each board is independent of the others in every consideration of economy and management. As a natural consequence, the rates and fares charged are in many cases greatly in excess of what we are accustomed to on this side the water, seriously restricting the interchange of productions and the energies of the people. In Scotland about one-sixth of the entire mileage of the empire produces one-ninth of the gross revenue, while in Ireland about one-seventh of the whole mileage produces only one-twentieth of the gross receipts; besides, whilst there is one mile of railway in Scotland for every 1460 persons, and one in England for every 2257 persons, in Ireland there is only one mile for every 3260 persons, so that Ireland is over 123 per cent. behind Scotland in this respect. I have the greatest possible objection to monopoly uncontrolled; but if unification of management and concentration of control do not involve monopoly, while experience has shown that they are indispensable to the success of railway enterprise, and that they act and react to the public advantage, I am therefore an advocate for concentration of management, because it secures and combines moderation in fares with profit to the shareholders.

It would be idle to point out what steam intercommunication has done for mankind in a thousand ways, and how important it is to devise means to increase its usefulness. I must be content with suggesting for consideration a few of the questions upon which I think railway reform and railway economy mainly depend.

It would be of no avail to refer to the waste of past expenditure in construction, except to say that the teachings of the past are the only safe guide to the policy of the future. As an engineer, I am proud to confess that our English railways, apart from the wastefulness, constitute a magnificent monument to the constructive talent of the age. But utility and economy, with due regard to safety, must now be studied above all other considerations. The palatial stations of Charing-cross and Cannon-street I admire as much as any one from an architectural point of view (although there is no more convenient, elegant, but unpretending, or cheaper metropolitan station than that at London-bridge, which cannot have cost but a very small fraction of either of the former), but I want to earn dividends for the shareholders, and to give the greatest accommodation to the public at the lowest possible remunerative rate. I do not hesitate to assert that the cost of no provincial railway should exceed 10,000*l.* per mile, including land, works, and plant, for a double line; but in many parts of England, and particularly in Ireland—where 60-mile velocities, for instance, are wholly out of the question—3000*l.* per mile should amply suffice for subsidiary single lines, including rolling stock, but exclusive of land, which I take for granted will freely be given for purposes so beneficial to the public, and advantageous to the landowners themselves. One remark I cannot help making here, with reference to the most gigantic and most improvident of all the metropolitan stations,—I mean that in course of erection for the Midland Railway, near King's-cross. This station, with its approaches, will cost a sum almost fabulous. I will only say that this outlay is a melancholy exhibition of railway extravagance, and that it goes far to explain the troubles into which railway enterprise has fallen. I believe this is the last erection of the kind that we are likely to see, and that the ambition of railway officials must, in the future, be confined to the prudent development of branch lines constructed upon a wholly new principle, which will render them a blessing instead of a reproach to our generation.

In making new railways, whether at home or in the colonies, the question of economical construction transcends all others in importance. I hold a strong opinion that the natural configuration of any country will, as a general rule, permit the working of railways upon what I shall here term the principle of surface construction, securing the public safety and convenience on the one hand, and a fair return for the capital invested on the other. Then, as to the question of maintenance,—it has never been properly treated, and it never will be honestly met so long as capital accounts remain open as a ready resource for every chairman out of which to bolster up dividends, and of every manager by which to maintain fictitious appearances. Had companies been kept face to face with only one source of supply, and that from revenue profits, they never could have fallen to their present depth of ruin and disaster. With an open credit, which we call capital, always at command, the opportunity, I may say the temptation, is ever present of debiting capital with all sorts of charges, which ought properly to have been placed against revenue. It is easy to conceive how, under such circumstances, directors of the highest honour and integrity have been led into errors which they now deplore; but their chief misfortune, in my opinion, has been the facility with which they have permitted themselves to be led away by officials with personal objects which do not appear to have harmonised with the true interests of the proprietary. All such charges as those for renewals of road, stock, and stations, ought undoubtedly to be charged to revenue without any reserve whatever; and I venture to think it would be well for a Society like this to devote some portion of its wide influence to making it clear beyond a question where the line should be drawn between capital and revenue. The closing of capital accounts is, I confess, no light matter in respect of existing companies. There can be no doubt that every new work of an original kind ought to be provided for by a special capital, if in itself of sufficient magnitude, and if not, in combination with other amounts, and in respect of any sudden or unlooked-for expenditure of any considerable sums for way, stock, or works, I would have the amount carried to a suspense account, the redemption to be spread over a reasonable period, and to be made out of surplus annual revenue. If this or some analogous system be not speedily adopted, it requires no soothsayer to predict what must happen : " Coming events cast their shadows before," and with regret I say, that before many years have passed away there will be but few solvent railway companies left. It is not only the difficulty they are now experiencing in their finances, but every day is ageing the entire of their property, which must be renewed and kept alive by an outlay which will tax the solvency and ability of the best of them. Everything connected with a railway is subject to the usual law of decay, every item has a certain life, whether it be taken in itself or forming part of a whole, whether rails, bridges, stations, plant, or anything connected with them, and although chargeable to revenue, I am not aware of any case where a redemption fund has been provided for these inevitable occurrences. In future, I would imperatively close every capital account of a new line with the authorisation of the Board of Trade permitting the line to be opened for public traffic; this of course implies the necessary and sufficient amount of rolling stock and stations. All else, not accompanied by the creation of new mileage, ought rigidly to go to the debit of revenue.

One word as to the mode which has recently been adopted of raising capital. The Brighton Company has on two occasions issued ordinary stock at 55 per cent. discount, thus saddling the concern for ever after with 100*l*. of liability for every 45*l.* received. This is the worst possible mode of raising money, because it more than doubles every expense attending the line, including employés, stores, maintenance, and renewals. This, I fear, will be no solitary instance. A much more rational way of meeting necessities would be the adoption of the system pursued by foreign governments, of contracting loans redeemable half-yearly, by drawing out a fixed percentage to be set aside from surplus profits. Working expenses are the first natural charge upon gross revenue; then interest upon debenture stock, which stock ought to be made perpetual, like the national debt; then should follow the formation of a fund for the half-yearly drawings to which I have referred, the share capital (preferential and ordinary) absorbing the remainder. There is not time to enlarge upon these views, nor do I claim the merit of novelty for them; but this statement will prove that in what I have further to say with respect to railway enterprise and management I have only two objects in view; one is to increase the security of the companies as investments of capital, and the other to assure the public that, notwithstanding the mistakes and the extravagances of a generation, the benefits of this indispensable aid to civilisation and progress may be secured fully and widely.

We now come to that which is no less important than all that has gone before—I mean the working of railways. We cannot recal the outlay of the past, but I firmly believe that even the most unfortunate railways can be redeemed by a wise and well-arranged system of working. I shall endeavour to show that revenues can be increased concurrent with a large reduction of expenses, and I would not be here this evening soliciting your attention unless I felt myself in a position to satisfy you how this can be done.

As to the revenue, I do not believe that railway managers, as a rule, trouble themselves to know the return derived from each train run as compared with the expense of the same. I would have a debtor and creditor account with every train despatched; showing on the one side the whole of the expenses incidental to it, and on the other the total amount earned.

The experience of the last thirty-five years provides us with very reliable figures of the cost of train mileage, in regard of every description of expenditure; and every train that would show a deficit in balancing the account should be unhesitatingly abandoned, excepting in such special cases as do not affect the general question.

I illustrate this in detail by a reference to the published accounts of the London and North-Western Railway Company, for the half-year ending June, 1866, which I have selected because it is comparatively low in the percentage of working expenses, and almost the best paying of all our railways. The gross earnings are at the rate of about 5s. per train per mile for passengers; and for merchandise 6s. 3¾d. To give shareholders the return to which they are justly entitled from this class of investment, I consider that the gross earnings necessary for this purpose ought not to be less than 7s. 6d. per mile for passenger trains at 20 miles speed, and increasing in amount to 10s. for 30 miles; 14s. for 40 miles; 20s. for 50 miles; and 30s. for 60 miles. It is absurd for companies to make so very little difference in their charge between high and low speeds as they do, knowing that whether in respect to the road, plant, or fuel, the cost increases in proportion to the velocity, and the charges should, therefore, be proportionate. I was much struck, when looking over the London and Brighton Railway accounts, to find that the gross earnings were under 4s. 10d. per train per mile; although, of my own knowledge, I am aware that many of their express trains, to and from Brighton, consist of some 20 carriages, each containing about 20 passengers, whose fares (allowing 25 per cent. for season-ticket holders) must realise not less than about 3*l.* per mile. It is clear, therefore, that the Brighton Company are running a large number of trains at a positive loss, else the average would not be so seriously reduced. If 4s. 10d. be a fair and remunerative rate (which it is not), no train should be run under that standard; and the maximum of 3*l.* per train mile is as much beyond what is necessary as the minimum is below it; the medium between the two to be arrived at, by an abandonment of all unpaying trains, would produce to the company a handsome accession to its revenue on the one hand, and permit of a large reduction in the charges to the public on the other. I may be told that the cutting off of the unremunerative trains would be an invasion of the public convenience; but the best test of this is the patronage bestowed on particular trains, and the neglect of others, which consequently do not pay. I am not forgetful that many of those unremunerative trains have been run, some from a spirit of rivalry, and some from a fear of competition; but rivalry must disappear in an effort to restore prosperity, and competition has found its level. Besides, the public are not so unreasonable as to expect that companies are to carry them without a proper return; the interests of both are identical, and neither is advantaged by a condition of things which has resulted in so much loss and misfortune. The expenditure part of the question is equally of vital importance, and I beg now to call attention to the amazing folly of railway engineers in overweighting the trains with that unnecessary and cumbersome appendage, the tender. The average gross weight of passenger trains may be stated at 70 tons; the average weight of a tender is over 25 per cent. of that, and invariably is over 200 per cent. in excess of the whole paying portion of the load carried. Now, when we know that not only is the tender costly, unnecessary, and cumbersome, but that the load of fuel and water which it conveys for supplying the engine can be made available for increasing the power and efficiency of the engine itself, I ask, what is to be thought of the persistency in continuing such an improvident system? There are at this moment working with great success on a Welsh railway engines with no tender, and where the fuel and water are in the highest degree conducive to the increase of power, economy, and safety. In their case the weight is distributed equally upon a large number of wheels, thus increasing the adhesion upon the rails, whilst the weight per wheel is proportionately reduced. (See Figs.

1, 2, and 3, the latter being section of Fig. 1, through bogie-pin, to show the pivoting centre.) These advantages must at once be apparent; and, I believe, will lead to an entire revolution in our locomotive arrangements;

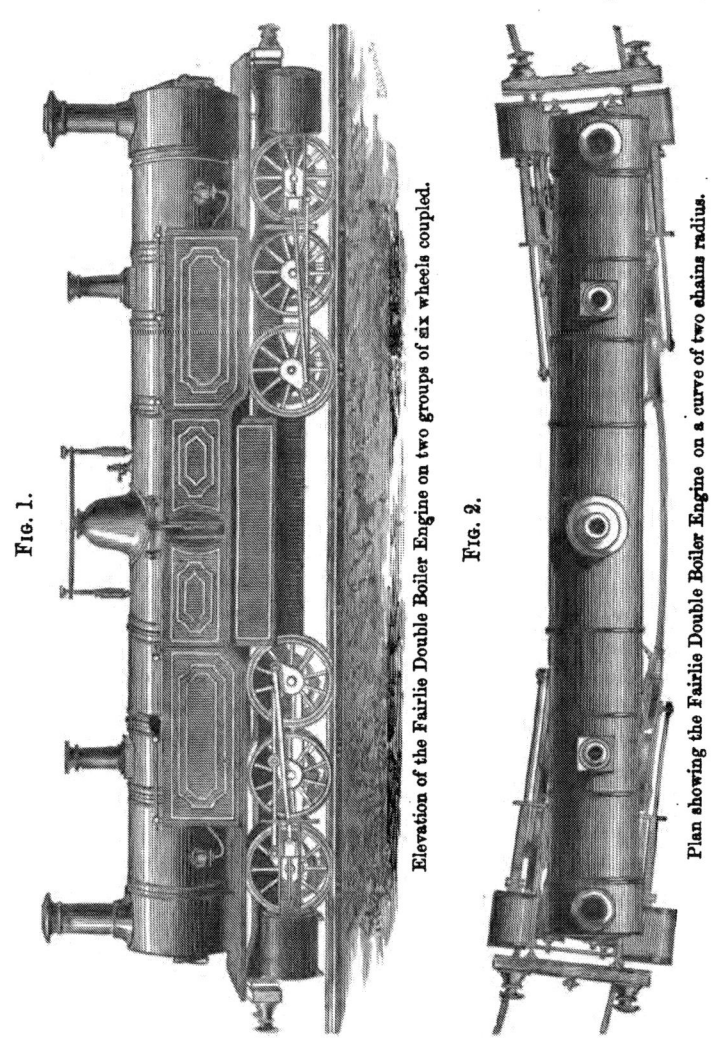

Fig. 1.
Elevation of the Fairlie Double Boiler Engine on two groups of six wheels coupled.

Fig. 2.
Plan showing the Fairlie Double Boiler Engine on a curve of two chains radius.

Fig. 3.

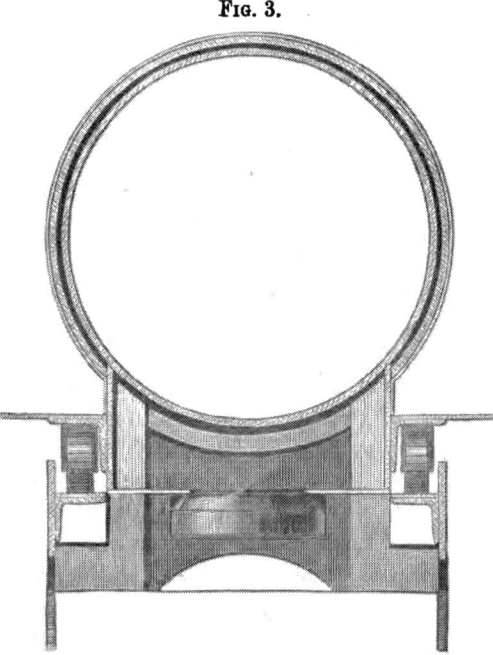

Enlarged tranverse section of engine through bogie-pin.

besides, the enormous economy which is effected in the maintenance of both engine and road is of the highest importance in the embarrassed condition of our railways. As respects the costs of tenders, and how they affect the dividends of railways, the following is given by way of illustration:—The London and North-Western Railway, which has the most uniform, and therefore the best paying merchandise traffic of any line in the kingdom, shows by its balance-sheet, already quoted, 7,333,371 tons of goods and minerals carried during that half-year, being about 46,800 tons net for each working day; the tare of this tonnage would not be less than a like amount, giving the gross tonnage per day at about 93,600. The average gross weight of each train, exclusive of the locomotive and tender, may fairly be set down at 300 tons;

therefore the number of trains per day would amount to 312, but from the fact, as stated in the balance-sheet, that the gross earnings of those trains per mile are under 6s. 4d., and taking the rate of freight at one penny per ton per mile, which it is believed is a correct average, we are able to estimate the paying load of each of those trains of 300 tons gross to be about 76 tons, or only 25 per cent., and thus we find that the number of trains per day must really be about 609, instead of 312. It is true that merchandise is composed of classes according to bulk and frailty, in many cases less than half a ton filling a wagon, and thus reducing the proportion of paying load to dead weight, but it is also true that in all such cases charges are made not only to pay for the full carrying weight of the wagon, but leaving ample margin to cover the risk of breakage in handling. The same balance-sheet shows that each net ton carried produces to the Company a sum of 4s. 7½d., which at a penny per ton per mile gives the average distance of each ton carried to be 55¼ miles; we have therefore 609 engines and tenders running 55½ miles every working day. Following this reasoning, let us see how doing away with the tender affects the question. Taking the tender to equal the weight of two loaded wagons, giving a net result of ten tons, and there being 609 in motion every day, it follows that their equivalent in net paying load would be about 6000 tons carried per day 55½ miles, which at the same average rate of one penny per ton per mile, gives the amount earnable from this source at 1387l. 10s. per day, and for 313 working days—representing one year—434,287l. 10s. We have been speaking of merchandise and mineral traffic only, but applying the same scrutiny to the figures of the passenger traffic (provided, of course, there were passengers to be carried), and substituting carriages for tenders of an equivalent weight, we should arrive at an income of a somewhat similar amount, both amounting to 868,575l. per annum net earnings, equal to a dividend of over 3 per cent. on the ordinary share capital. It is well known that the cost of maintenance of tenders is fully as much, if not more than that of the carriages or wagons which are suggested for substitution.

The method of conducting passenger traffic yielding so little per train per mile, is of such importance, and the discrepancy between remunerative and unremunerative weights hauled, is so irrational and glaring, that it deserves to be considered a little more in detail. Still, quoting from the London and North-Western Railway balance-sheet, it appears that the gross produce of 9,613,195 passengers is 1,280,507l., or under 2s. 8d. per passenger. Taking the average rate for each at 1½d. per mile, this gives 21 miles as the distance travelled by each, whilst the gross earnings per mile of passenger trains are about 5s., which, at a like rate of 1½d. per mile, shows that the average number of passengers per train per mile is 40; allowing for a considerable amount of luggage to each passenger, this number could not be estimated at more than four tons. Now four tons is neither more nor less than about one-twelfth of the weight of the locomotive engine and tender (the tender alone being about five times this weight), and taking the passenger trains at say 50 tons, the paying load will bear not more than one-twenty-fourth part of the gross weight of each train. It is evident, therefore, that the paying is altogether out of proportion to the unpaying load; although it is admitted that on railways such as the London and North-Western, from the circumstances of the great length and numerous unprofitable branches, there must always exist a much larger proportion of dead to paying weight than is the case with lines with no such encumbrances. Now, there is no reason whatever why the present disproportion should exist, or anything like it.

This is no new subject with men who have given their serious and unprejudiced attention to it. I find that in 1849 Professor Gordon, an engineer of considerable eminence, expressed, in a very able pamphlet called "Railway Economy," similar views to those which I have advanced. In page 4, he says: "The existing railway machinery will be found to be monstrously disproportionate to the useful effect produced in four-fifths of the number of times that the machine is put in action. And to this waste of power may be most justly attributed much of the present embarrassment of railway companies."

The judicious despatch of trains, and the proportion of paying to unpaying loads, are two of the most important subjects connected with railway management. These, however, could be grappled with at any time by a really competent man, so as to enormously increase the net result even with existing stock; but there are the difficulties which always surround independent departmental control, exhibiting on all occasions a strange unwillingness to adopt any change which shall interfere with their preconceived opinions, or occasion trouble or thought in departing from a system which one is tempted to think has its own personal peculiar advantages. It seems never to have occurred to these gentlemen that in the discharge of their important duties, involving every consideration they can bring to them, in the interest of their employers, what a close relation there is between the question of the dead weight necessary to the efficiency of the traffic and the dividends to those who have entrusted them with their important functions.

The Metropolitan Railway is, without exception, one of the greatest engineering triumphs of the age, being one of the cases where cost, it would seem, has been of secondary consideration; but, certainly, its management cannot be commended, and time will not permit of dealing with the general question. The magnitude of the traffic is evinced by the fact that during the half-year ending December, 1867, nearly twelve millions of passengers were carried over the line by 348 trains on week-days and 212 on Sundays, averaging over 328 trains per day throughout the year. The distance run by each of these trains is understood to be $4\frac{1}{4}$ miles, consequently the train miles per day are over 1396. By dividing the actual number of passengers, 11,916,924, carried for the half-year by the number of days in the same period, we obtain 65,298 passengers carried per day, which, in 328 trains, is 198 passengers per train. This number of passengers per train for the entire distance run—say 4¼ miles—would give an average of less than 47 passengers per mile. This, however, is not the case, because the gross earnings per train mile being under 9s. 4d., the amount chargeable per passenger per mile would require to be about $2\tfrac{4}{10}$d. This would be above the average rate charged. It is, however, impossible to find out from the company's balance-sheet what the real average is. To arrive at something like an average, I take 100 passengers, 50 single and 50 return journeys, from Moorgate-street to all stations, and divide these into 20 first-class, 30 second-class, and 50 third-class, which will give the average rate per passenger at 2·02d., and this divided into 9s. 4d. gives a little over 55 passengers per train per mile. The trains on this line are mostly composed of five carriages, weighing about 16 tons each, and one locomotive, weighing 42 tons, together 122 tons. Thus we have 122 tons of train weight to carry an average of 55 passengers, which at 14 to the ton is under 4 tons, being only one ton of paying load to 30 tons of dead weight. Some objection may be taken to this mode of dealing with figures. It will be said the average number of passengers given to each mile cannot be considered as the exact number travelling that distance. This is no doubt so, but it cannot materially affect the question, for if the whole average of 198 passengers travelled 1¼ mile, there would be none the remaining 3 miles; the only difference in the proportion of paying to unpaying load which could arise from this would be a slight increase of the former to the latter for 1¼ mile only, while for the 3 miles it would be wholly dead load. To prove the correctness of this calculation, we have only to assume what many might be disposed to imagine, that 198 passengers instead of 55 are carried per train per mile, the result would give 101,293,854 instead of nearly 24,000,000 now carried.

Nothing could be more appropriately said at this moment than the following quotation from Professor Gordon's pamphlet, written twenty years ago. At page 24 he says:—" These figures indicate the small portion of the mechanism of the railway system of transport that is actually brought into requisition even on the most frequented lines. Thousands, nay, millions, of miles are run by locomotives and carriages on the present system, whilst they are performing an amount of transport of passengers preposterously disproportioned to the power and capacity of the trains employed for effecting it."

Contrast this condition of things on the Metropolitan Railway with our ordinary omnibus traffic. We find that the omnibus, which has to travel over an infinitely worse road than any line, weighs somewhere about one ton, whilst it carries 28 passengers or two tons, thus giving a proportion of two tons of paying to one ton of unpaying load; but as we have included the weight of the horse, *i.e.*, the locomotive engine in the calculation on the metropolitan working, it is but fair to include the horses which haul the omnibus. Two horses with every equipment cannot weigh a ton, consequently, at the very outside, the proportion is one to one, or one ton of paying load to one ton of material employed to convey it. These are very suggestive facts; they have surprised me; and that this line has earned any dividend at all under these circumstances proves its enormous productive capability. Beyond the question of proportion of effective to non-effective duty, let us consider how it all bears on the maintenance of the railway stock and road, and how they are affected thereby. I have already given the weights of the locomotives and carriages, the former at 42 and the latter at 16 tons each.

The carriages have very long wheel bases, consequently they offer great resistance to the tractive force of the engine, besides being very injurious to the rails rounding the curves.

The engines have 32 tons on 4 wheels, or 16 tons per pair. We have only to imagine this enormous weight ploughing along at 30 miles an hour to form some idea of the destructive effect, not only to the rails, but to the substructure and the machines, the effect being destructive alike to all. No wonder that the line has, as it is stated, been relaid in many places three times with steel rails since it opened five years ago. Not content with this rate of destruction to road and stock, the Metropolitan Company are now receiving, or about to receive, locomotive engines of a still more destructive character to work the St. John's-wood branch, weighing 45 tons on 6 wheels, with a wheel base of 14 feet. The only approach to a saving feature in the 42-ton engines—viz., carrying the leading end of the engine on a Bissel truck with four wheels —is in these new engines omitted. The Bissel arrangement does to some extent reduce the enormous friction of the engines on rounding the curves, notwithstanding which the grating and grinding noise of the wheels can be heard at a considerable distance. The spirit of rivalry between armour plates and guns is reproduced in steel rails and locomotive engines, with this difference, that the armour plates can be made to withstand the power of the heaviest guns, whilst steel rails cannot withstand the battering of these 45-ton steam hammer locomotive engines.

The destructive element of the ordinary type of locomotive is so vital, and affects the question of shareholders' dividends so much, that I would fain trespass on the time of the meeting to show how this results. The superstructure or principal weight of a locomotive engine borne on six wheels is supported on six points close to and inside each wheel. Between these supports and the wheel the carrying springs are placed. Now a very heavy engine with a great amount of overhang must, from the imperfections of the road, rock about a great deal, and the centre of gravity of the engine, instead of moving forward in a straight line, as it should do if the line and everything connected with it were perfect,

Fig. 4.

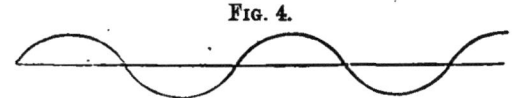

Showing the line traversed by the centre of gravity to each side of centre line of motion through the deflecting action of the springs.

forms a continuous line of curves and reverse curves on each side of the line of direction, as represented in Fig. 4.

This is caused at first by some defect or slight obstruction in the road, and is afterwards kept up by the springs receiving and deflecting with the force of the up-and-down movement of the great body of weight resting on them, as shown in Fig. 5.

Fig. 5.

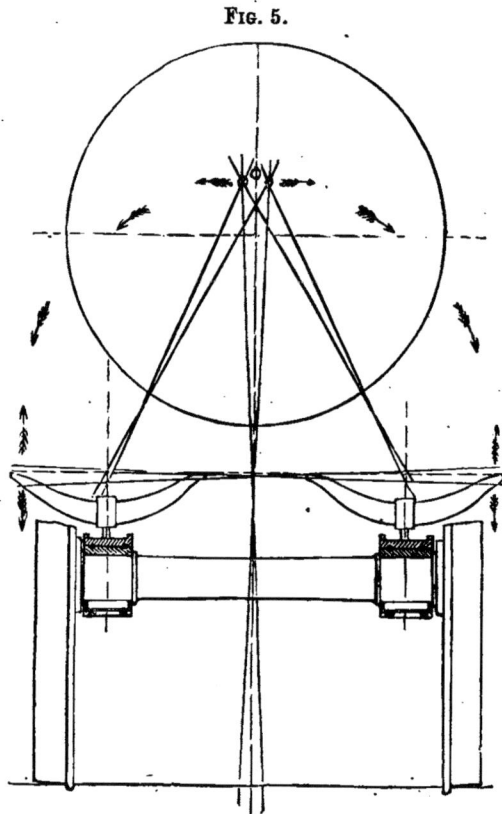

Showing the lateral movement of the centre of gravity to each side of the centre line of motion caused by the vertical action of the springs; showing also the deflecting action of the spring, and how it affects the centre of gravity; caused by an imperfect permanent way.

29

This action of the springs is caused by the oscillation of the centre of gravity to either side of the centre line of motion (see Fig. 5), and then easing themselves by flinging the weight from one to the other, either diagonal to, or at right angles with, the line of motion, and so repeated until the oscillations are gradually diminished; but it is found in practice that the oscillations never cease, for before one set is completely reduced another commences, keeping up a constant surging or soughing from side to side during the entire journey. The exact force of impact on the rail caused in this manner is represented by the amount of deflection of each spring beyond its normal condition. We shall be well within the mark by saying the destructive effect to the rail is over 60 per cent. more than the normal load on the wheels. Thus, in the case of the 45-ton Metropolitan engines, it is not simply this weight divided over six wheels, but a concussion of 60 per cent. in addition, or between 11 and 12 tons blow on the rails. Herein we find the explanation of the frequent necessity for the renewal of the rails. It is often argued that, because the additional load is received, taken up, and afterwards thrown off by each spring, the damaging effect on the rails is very little beyond that of the normal load, but I submit that this is not so. On the contrary, whatever extra force is thrown on a spring by momentum to flatten it beyond its normal condition, that extra force passes to the rail—not, however, as the blow of a hammer, as in that case the line of motion of the centre of gravity would be represented as in Fig. 6, but as a

Fig. 6.

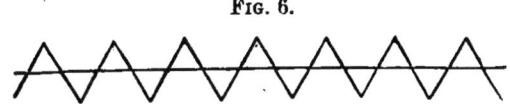

Showing the line that would be traversed by the centre of gravity to each side of the centre line of motion if there were no springs, each angle representing the blow of a hammer on the rails.

load graduated from its normal condition according to the

velocity of the wheels and the time taken up by the springs in their action of deflection and return, better represented, perhaps, by a double inclined plane. (See Fig. 7.)

The best practical illustration I can offer to the meeting upon all these points of mechanical engineering is to invite

FIG. 7.

Double-inclined plane, showing how the concussion or blow is given to the rails beyond the normal or fixed load on the wheels; caused by oscillation.

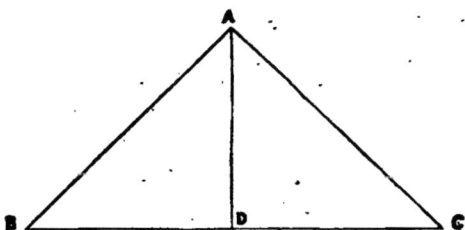

B to A is a plane representing the deflection or downward action of the spring.
A to C is a plane representing the return of the spring to its normal position.
A to D represents the greatest deflection of spring, usually amounting to from 30 to 75 per cent. beyond the normal load of six tons on the wheel.
B to C distance traversed on periphery of wheel during time taken up by the spring in its action of deflexion and return to its normal position.

attention to the models and drawings before it of an engine which has been specially designed to meet the objections we have just been discussing. The engine does not exist as a mere abstract idea, but is daily in operation on the Neath and Brecon Railway; and within the last few days one of them, which has been working over two years, has undergone a severe test in the presence of several eminent engineers, who, in consequence, have accorded it their warmest approval, several of whom I have the pleasure to see here this evening, and who may probably be disposed to describe their own experience.

The engines are remarkable for the almost total absence of oscillation, and the graceful ease with which they run round the very sharpest curves is matter of surprise to all who have ridden on them; the sense of safety experienced when on the engine is irresistible, and the motion is so pleasantly unlike that of the ordinary engines, that it has been described by Captain Tyler, of the Board of Trade, as giving the sensation of flying, and by others as that of sailing in smooth water. In corroboration of this, it may not be considered out of place here to quote a passage from the report of Captain Tyler and Mr. Eboral, who have lately returned from an inspection of the Grand Trunk Railway of Canada. In page 44, after giving a full description of the locomotive engines in use on that line, the report says, " The class of engine best suited to the climate, and for the various circumstances of the case, would, I have no doubt, be an engine running on two bogie trucks, each provided with a pair of cylinders, and four-wheeled or six-wheeled, according to the work required— and without a tender. Such an engine would be peculiarly safe to travel over a winter road; would combine a minimum wear and tear to itself and the rails, with a maximum of adhesion, and would be the most effective and most economical that the company could employ. I had the opportunity some time ago of testing engines of this description on the Neath and Brecon Railway, designed by Mr. Fairlie, and have found the principle to be good, though certain points of detail required improvement. Such engines are also in use for the sharp curves and steep gradients of the Queensland Railway."

These engines have developed a relative power equal to two of the engines employed for hauling the goods trains on the London and North-Western Railway, whilst the destructive effect on the rails, road, and engine, is greatly reduced. The employment of such engines would enable companies to double the carrying capacity of their lines without necessitating any additional outlay, and therefore they are especially valuable in the case of single lines. There are those who might consider it inexpedient to increase the present dimensions of goods trains, and in that case the engines would be too powerful, but the point is met by their permitting a very large reduction to be made in the weight per wheel, amounting to so much as one-half that on the ordinary engine wheels, while its power remains equal to the best of them. It will therefore be readily understood that the life of the wheel tyres and rails would be greatly prolonged. Companies like the London and North-Western, having reached, it is supposed, the maximum of load per train, have been driven to the costly expedient of triplicating their lines of rails for great distances. I venture to think that this immense outlay could have been avoided by the use of engines better adapted to the exigencies of an over-crowded traffic, whilst at the same time assuring a saving in haulage labour of nearly one-half, together with a most appreciable saving in fuel.

I have spoken of the Metropolitan Railway and its enormous traffic. That is but a portion of the prodigious traffic of the metropolis and its suburbs. This description of traffic should be treated in altogether a different manner to the main provincial lines. The Metropolitan should be conducted by stock giving the minimum of dead weight with the maximum of efficiency; this, I think, could be best done by what may be termed steam omnibuses, made to carry say 60 passengers, but with power sufficient to haul additional carriages during the busiest hours of the day—in the middle or slack time the omnibuses could alone carry the mean average of passengers. The weight of the entire machine, together with its load of passengers, would be less than that of the present locomotive engine alone. I have brought here to-night the drawing of a steam carriage, designed expressly for conducting the traffic of the proposed cheap lines in Ireland, which will be useful to show you the character of steam omnibuses (to be modified to suit circumstances) I should recommend for working metropolitan lines. This carriage would work with efficiency and economy the line over Mount Cenis. (See Fig. 8.)

Before closing this paper—already, I fear, too long—I desire to do justice to a gentleman, Mr. James Samuel, who, when engineer to the Eastern Counties Railway, successfully

Fig. 8.

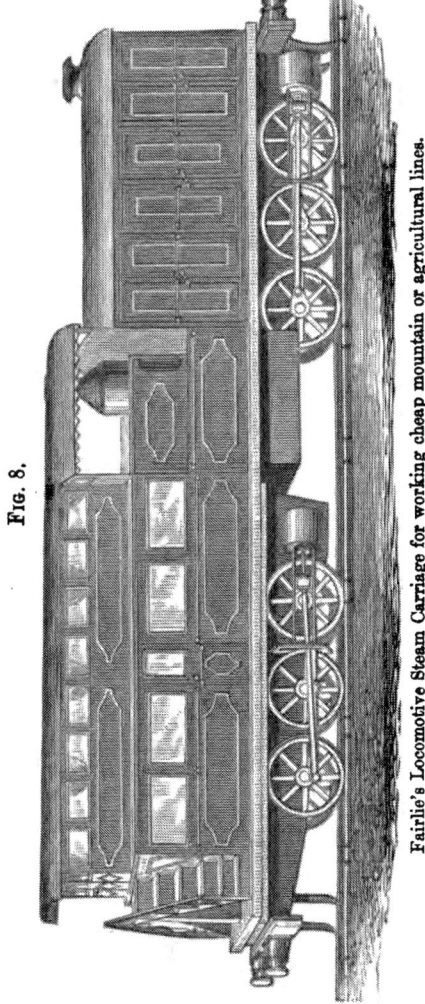

Fairlie's Locomotive Steam Carriage for working cheap mountain or agricultural lines.

put in practice on that line very much the system of locomotive which I advocate now for metropolitan and branch lines. Mr. Samuel worked his invention for some time between

Printed by Libri Plureos GmbH in Hamburg, Germany